# Sharing Your Love Story

## A Woman's Guide on When, Where and How to Share the Gospel

Marlaine Peachey

WESTBOW
PRESS®
A DIVISION OF THOMAS NELSON
& ZONDERVAN

WestBow Press books may be ordered through booksellers or by contacting:

WestBow Press
A Division of Thomas Nelson & Zondervan
1663 Liberty Drive
Bloomington, IN 47403
www.westbowpress.com
1 (866) 928-1240

Because of the dynamic nature of the Internet, any web addresses or links contained in this book may have changed since publication and may no longer be valid. The views expressed in this work are solely those of the author and do not necessarily reflect the views of the publisher, and the publisher hereby disclaims any responsibility for them.

This book is a work of non-fiction. Unless otherwise noted, the author and the publisher make no explicit guarantees as to the accuracy of the information contained in this book and in some cases, names of people and places have been altered to protect their privacy.

Any people depicted in stock imagery provided by Getty Images are models, and such images are being used for illustrative purposes only. Certain stock imagery © Getty Images.

Scripture quotations, unless otherwise indicated, are taken from The Holy Bible, New International Version®, NIV® Copyright © 1973, 1978, 1984, 2011 by Biblica, Inc.® Used by permission. All rights reserved worldwide.

Scripture quotations marked NASB are taken from The New American Standard Bible®, Copyright © 1960, 1962, 1963, 1968, 1971, 1972, 1973, 1975, 1977, 1995 by The Lockman Foundation. Used by permission.

ISBN: 978-1-9736-5306-6 (sc)
ISBN: 978-1-9736-5307-3 (hc)
ISBN: 978-1-9736-5305-9 (e)

Library of Congress Control Number: 2019901315

Print information available on the last page.

WestBow Press rev. date: 02/19/2019

# Contents

# $\mathcal{D}$edication

This book is dedicated to all who are led by The Spirit and heed the Great Commission:

*"Write down the revelation and make it plain on tablets so that a herald may run with it. For the revelation awaits an appointed time."* Habbakuk 2:2

# *Introduction*

*Sharing the gospel in today's world may seem a daunting task to some, but when you take a closer look at Whose job it really is and what needs to be said, the burden is lifted and the commission becomes an adventure. It is an honor and privilege to introduce Christ to someone and you should "always be prepared to give an answer to everyone who asks you, to give the reason for the hope that you have" (1 Peter 3:15).*

*But when, where and how? This study will guide you in each of these areas, by simplifying your words, studying the truth, learning how to be led by The Spirit, knowing and understanding those you meet, engaging them to discipleship, making yourself available to Christ and the assignment set before you.*

*At this very moment, there are people yet unsaved who are longing and eager to fill the emptiness in their hearts. If you are a willing vessel, God will use your love story to change their lives forever.*

# Chapter 1

# What's Your Story?

$\mathcal{S}$o......what's your story?

Yes, you have one. Everybody does.

Everyone that knows Jesus, that is.

And if you know Jesus, you know He loves stories. After all, He inspired the most famous book ever written. It's been a best seller for years. The Bible contains many life stories that fall under a variety of genres, some of which include drama, action, miracles, murder, passion and best of all redemption. Regardless of how great or small, all lead to the revelation of Who He is. Therefore, every story is important, even yours. We all belong to His family and we all play a part.

Your story was meant to give glory to God. And He has commissioned you to tell it. The problem is some of us don't think we are good story tellers, or we don't feel our story carries much weight in the kingdom. Others are simply afraid to share.

I will never forget the first live testimony I ever heard. I had just accepted Christ and went to a Christian women's luncheon. I knew I was going to hear someone talk of Jesus and how He changed their life. I was excited to witness in person for the first time, someone speaking to a room full of ladies, leading them to Christ. I was prepared to hear an endearing, heartwarming account. Surprisingly, after being introduced, the guest speaker, seated at the head table, rolled herself over to the podium in the wheelchair she had been sitting in. No one had noticed it. I quickly assumed she had conquered some handicap or was on the road to recovery from a debilitating illness. I wasn't expecting what I heard. As her story unfolded, I learned that this remarkable lady was evidently getting her hair done in a building in downtown New Orleans. The building suddenly caught on fire and she had no way to exit but to jump from eight stories. She said God (her Savior) was with her and she lived to tell about it. I don't know how long some of us sat there in silence with our mouths gaping open after she finished. Many had signed comment cards and said they accepted Christ for the first time. There was a long line of people waiting to speak with her afterward.

As much as I was in awe of such a miracle, my own story of simply praying the sinner's prayer on the floor of my den seemed to pale in comparison. I had never escaped a flaming building, I have never been healed from an incurable disease nor had I had a near death experience and passed through a tunnel of light. That day I wanted to hear more of Jesus' miracles, but sharing my experience was shoved to the back burner. I didn't see myself as a storyteller, or the phone ringing off the hook with requests for speaking engagements.

Instead, I spent a lot of time in those early years on my sofa curled up with my Bible and a cup of coffee as soon as the kids got on the school bus. After my first sip, the hot piping brew was often forgotten in the still, quiet of my home as I poured through my Bible and drank in story after story of God's love that I was reading for the first time. I miss those days! Just me, sitting at Jesus' feet and learning like a small child.

I began to realize salvation came to people in many ways, not just exceptional ones. Every testimony glorified God and taught me more about Him. Hours would pass as I read stories of mercy, provision, healing and favor as well as the heartbreak of many betraying God Himself. I began to marvel that I was no different than anyone I had read about. I had received mercy, provision and favor, as well as healing in my heart. I too had betrayed Him. But just like them, I had been prompted by the Holy Spirit to come to Christ.

I began to see myself in a different light. I wasn't Queen Esther, or even the Queen of Sheba, but I had become a child of God. The God who sent His Son to die for me, now lived *in* me. I learned He loves me more than I can imagine and wants me to tell others of His love. He wants you to do the same.

So, let's get back to you. Your testimony can take less than a minute or go on for a longer time, but if you know the main point, even the fewest words can convey volumes. The best example was given by a man named Bartimaeus in the Bible. He was once asked by the elders to tell his story. He responded with, "I only know once I was blind, but now I see." Wow, talk about powerful. Bart's few but clear words have been quoted again and again and essentially, they are true for all of us. Once we were blind, but after accepting Christ, we all discovered the truth.

So, what's your story? As I said, let's discover your main focal point – you know, the crux of your story. Keep it simple......say, did you know crux is Latin for cross? That ought to give you an idea of where we are going.

We all have a story of arriving at the foot of the cross in some way and God brought us there individually.

Let's begin with the following exercises:

Exercise 1: Write your salvation story in one sentence. That may sound impossible, but if you were asked to give your story in one sentence as the blind man did, write down the brass tacks here. Let me give you an example. My story is "I believed I had to work my way to heaven, but I found out my Savior paid for it in full." What is your bottom line? Write it here:

_____

_____

_____

_____

_____

_____

_____

_____

Exercise 2: Shorten it even more. How short can you make
that sentence? Here's my example: "Jesus paid the price for
me." Let's see how short you can get yours:

_____

_____

_____

_____

_____

_____

_____

Now you have the basis of your story. When you share, you might be called on to give different aspects or part of it, but your bottom line will all come down to that one short sentence. That's your story!! There is no right or wrong answer in the exercises above except for one thing. Your story should always point to Him, not you. The long one might have included you, but the second one should be about Him. If not, try again.

Did you ever think your testimony could fit on a t-shirt? I'm not saying go run out and get one, I'm just saying words can be powerful. God said "Let there be light" and there was light. He didn't read a proclamation. I can say "Jesus paid the price for me" and it will bring light to someone's heart. In the appendix of this book, I will help you develop your story.

Here in Chapter 1, I want you to know yours in the simplest way. No matter how long I have been given to talk, it always comes back to that basic fact of Exercise 2. And at times, it's all I have had to say.

Now that wasn't hard, was it?

Truth be told, in this day and age, it's badly needed. There are people who are hurting and without hope. They need to know Him and if we are ready and available, God will let us know when and where to tell our story; we only have to listen to His prompting. Your gift may not be evangelism, it may be helping, encouraging or giving. But even evangelists are called to help, encourage and give. We are all part of one body. And if you are called to share, you need to be obedient. You may never know the impact you have had on others until you get to heaven. Now that we have your basic story down, let's talk about His.

## Class Discussion:

1. Ask class members to share their story in shortened form. Discuss the differences or similarities everyone has in those few words.

2. Did anyone have a problem getting to the point?

3. Discuss stories you have heard that touched your hearts. What was the main point? Was God glorified?

4. What is your favorite story of salvation in the Bible and why?

# Chapter 2

# What's His Story?

*S*ome of you might wonder why I am including this chapter. After all, if you are sharing your love story, shouldn't you already know His? Is this really necessary?

If you are joined in marriage to someone for a number of years, you know them very well (or you should) even though situations change and time may prove you wrong. Unlike man, God never changes. He is the same yesterday, today and forever. His steadfast love never ceases and His mercies are new every morning. What a wonderful, faithful God we serve. He is forgiving, just, merciful, holy, ever present and all powerful. There is none like Him.

I have listened to many love stories on my life journey. Once in a while, I come across one which is attributed to our Lord, but contains characterizations contrary to His nature or offers facts that are totally unscriptural. The person speaking has had a spiritual experience, but because of lack of knowledge, regales dramatically with facts that go against the truth. God may do something different in someone else's life, but He never contradicts Himself.

Many of you have been taught the truth your whole life and can't even imagine this happening. Others might not pick up on an untruth or thought it minor or unimportant and credit the story as giving glory to God, but after spending hour after hour studying in my early days, I recognize it immediately. It curls my toes.

The point I am making is this: if you are going to share truth you must know truth. Jesus said "I am the truth." If you truly know Him, you must know the truth.

Are you aware of how government experts recognize fraudulent money? You would think they spend hours "learning every trick in the book" a counterfeit artist might attempt. But that would take an exhaustive study and new methods are invented all the time. That's not how it's done. Instead, trained specialists focus all their efforts on studying only the real thing in every detail. They know every mark, every part of the design, down to the hairs on Benjamin Franklin's head. As a result, when any fake is placed before them, the forgery stands out like a sore thumb.

*This chapter is not about looking for errors in love stories. It's meant to make sure nothing but the truth goes into yours.*

Let's go over the story of salvation and scriptures that support these truths. Take time to look up each one.

| Story of Salvation | Scripture |
| --- | --- |
| *God is perfect; with Him there is no sin at all.* | *Psalm 18:30* |
| *He cannot abide with sin.* | *Habakkuk 1:13a* |
| *He created the heavens and the earth.* | *Genesis 1:1* |
| *He created man in His own image.* | *Genesis 1:27* |
| *He fellowshipped with them. (Adam and Eve)* | *Genesis 3:8* |
| *They sinned and broke fellowship with God.* | *Genesis 3:22-24* |
| *God's plan was to send His Son to restore fellowship.* | *1 John 4:10* |
| *Blood had to be shed, or there was no forgiveness.* | *Hebrews 9:22* |
| *We could not pay the price ourselves.* | *Psalm 49:7* |

| | |
|---|---|
| *The old sacrificial system was temporary.* | *Hebrews 9:1-10* |
| *Jesus came to save us.* | *Hebrews 9:15* |
| *He fulfilled every prophecy.* | *Romans 10:4* |
| *He died once and for all as the perfect lamb.* | *Hebrews 9:12* |
| *When He died, He said "It is finished."* | *John 10:30* |
| *He was buried and rose again from the dead.* | *1 Corinthians 15:4* |
| *He offers us the gift of eternal life.* | *John 3:16* |
| *All who receive Him, are born into His family.* | *John 1:12* |
| *He lives within us; working out our lives.* | *Philippians 2:13* |
| *One day He will return; we will live with Him forever.* | *Hebrews 9:28* |

During the time I was learning, it was difficult to "unbelieve" things I was wrongly taught as a child. One night I was struggling with an issue and in frustration, I went to my room and threw myself across the bed in the dark. The only light in the room was the time glowing in red numbers from an LED clock beside the bed. It was 8:31. I still had to put the kids to bed and it was getting late, but this was important. In desperation, I said, "Lord, I'm learning so much I never knew. And to be perfectly honest, I'm having a hard time letting go of some things I believed to be true all my life and your Word says they are not."

Time passed as I lay there, pondering the issue I addressed to God. I believed He heard me, but nothing really came to me, or so I thought. It was getting late. I glanced back to check the time and discovered it was still 8:31. Impossible! Was the clock broken? I looked at it again and suddenly it dawned on me the numbers looked like a scripture verse: 8:31. I waited longer; still no change. I said, "God, are you showing me something? Wow! But if that is a scripture verse, I have no idea what book it is in!" I had been all over the Word lately, studying like I was preparing a thesis. Then the thought came to me that my friends always said if you are going to read the Bible, begin with the Gospel of John. With excited anticipation, I ran to my den and opened my Bible to John 8:31. Here's what I found. The words were in red, (Jesus speaking):

**"If you hold to my teaching, you are really my disciples.
Then you will know the truth, and
the truth will set you free."**

Just as he spoke to the Jews 2000 years ago, His Word was fresh for me that night. Never again would I settle for anyone's else's words, anyone's else's doctrine, anyone else's so called truths, but His and His alone for the rest of my life.

Perhaps you may know who He is, but never understood before what His sacrifice accomplished, or that He paid the price for you. You might have had a "spiritual experience" but have never accepted Him as Savior and turned your life over to Him. Maybe you have asked Him into your heart, but never gave Him all of your life. Are you still hanging on to the controls? When you come into a relationship with Christ, he comes not only as Savior, but Lord of your life.

First and foremost, you have to believe in Him. Salvation is based on faith, not on your own works, Ephesians 2:8 says, "For it is by grace you have been saved, through faith—and this is not from yourselves, it is the gift of God— not by works, so that no one can boast."

If you have never totally trusted in Jesus Christ for your salvation, and you desire to make Him Lord of your life, say this prayer:

> *"God, I believe in you. I believe Jesus came and died for my sins and rose again from the dead. I am sorry for all my sins. Please forgive me and come into my life. Be my Savior and Lord. I will follow you all the days of my life. Thank you for the gift of eternal life. In Jesus name, Amen."*

For those of you who just received Him for the first time, welcome into the family of God!! Begin spending time with Him reading your Bible and learning more about truth. Make sure you attend a church that believes in the inerrant Word of God.

For those of you who already knew it well, HIS story is never too old to tell. You may think "the whole world knows it" but always remember that you may be sharing the story fresh to someone who has never heard or understood it. I know; I was one of them and there are many, many more.

I have been asked to include the "Roman Road" in this study which is a tool many use to witness for Christ. You will find that in the Appendix of this book.

Now that we have our stories straight, let's answer the questions below and move on to the next chapter.

Class Discussion:

1. Ask if someone would like to share an example of when they learned truth for the first time.

2. How important is it to stay in the Word?

3. Which part of the salvation story do you find most interesting?

4. How do you handle a situation where someone shares an untruth? Look up Galatians 6:1 and discuss.

5. Go back over the scriptures above and ask class members for others verses they know that support the statements.

# Chapter 3

# Who's in Charge?

*N*ow that you have your story and His story down pat, I'm sure you know what to do next.

Not exactly.

Where do we go in the world to spread the gospel? Who wants to hear our story anyway? Does anyone really care? God forbid, we could be sent to a foreign country among terrorists! Are we going to be released into a possible den of lions and expected to survive, succeed and return victor? What if someone asks to hear our love story and it's just to criticize or trap us? Who signed us up for this anyway?

Relax. It's not your job.

Ok, so it's God's. Sure, I've read the Bible and know where some have ended up regardless. The fear is overwhelming. I suddenly feel totally fulfilled carpooling the kids. It must be true: don't ever discuss politics or religion.

No problem. God isn't about religion.

How can you possibly say God isn't "religious"? That's ridiculous.

Religion is man's attempt to reach God on his own efforts. God never established religion. He offers an opportunity for relationship. That's what this is about. Your love story is about your relationship with God. Who doesn't love a good love story?

How can I be sure who to talk to, what to say? How can I be sure I can convince them of the truth?

Again, it's not your job. Nothing you say will convince anyone. You cannot change a heart, only God can. Jesus explained it's the Holy Spirit's job to convict someone, not yours.

You mean it's not up to me?

No, the Holy Spirit is in charge of who, where, when and how you should witness. You should be led by the Spirit. If you are moving on your own gumption, well, then you really are on your own.

Exactly what will the Holy Spirit do?

Here is a list of some of His works. It will make you feel a lot better.

| Works of the Holy Spirit | Scripture |
|---|---|
| *He will dwell in you.* | *John 14:16-17* |
| *He will teach you all things.* | *John 14:26a* |
| *He will help you to remember verses you need.* | *John 14:26b* |
| *He will tell you what to say.* | *John 16:13-15* |
| *He will reveal to you what you need to know.* | *1 Corinthians 2 9-16* |
| *He will testify to the Truth.* | *John 15:26* |
| *It is His job to convict the world.* | *John 16:8* |
| *Do not worry what to say.* | *Matthew 10:18-20* |
| *He will give you strength to speak.* | *Acts 1:8* |
| *He anoints you to speak and will be with you.* | *1 John 2, 20,27* |
| *We are not our own.* | *1 Corinthians 6:9* |
| *He will help us.* | *Romans 8:26-27* |
| *We need to be led by the Spirit.* | *Romans 8:14-16* |
| *We need to walk in the Spirit.* | *Galatians: 22-25* |

Wow! That certainly is a lot! But what if I say what I am led to say, do what I am led to do, and they still reject me?

Jesus said in Luke 10:16, ""The one who listens to you listens to Me, and the one who rejects you rejects Me; and he who rejects Me rejects the One who sent Me." Don't take it to heart; it is Him they are rejecting. You are just the messenger. Does that make you feel better?

Yes. But it doesn't make me happy that someone will reject Christ.

It is unlikely that you will be the only person in the world God will use to bring them to Him. He wants none of us to perish and will send another and another. All you have to do is be led by the Spirit and obey.

Well, that takes a lot off my mind and my shoulders. I can loosen up.

Not exactly. We should always be alert, listening to the Spirit if He calls on us. Sometimes it could be just a word, not our whole story. Sometimes it can be unplanned and on the spur of the moment or to someone you don't even know. And sometimes you will be called to witness without a word. It will be your actions and the Holy Spirit will talk to them Himself. It can also be totally something uncanny to you, but just what someone needs at the moment. Could you be that open to the Spirit?

Wow. Where do I start?

Pray, listen and be available. Then, follow through and be obedient.

You make it sound so easy.

This is God's business, His plan, and He never fails. Trust Him and simply do what he says: "Follow me!"

Feel better?

Yes!!

## Class Discussion:

1. Who's in Charge?

2. What is our job in this?

3. How do we handle rejection?

4. How can we make sure we are following the Spirit?

5. What if nothing happens after I was led to witness. What do I do?

6. Did I do it wrong?

# Chapter 4

## Draw Near

*A* full-time job in the working world today can zap the tar out of you (This includes mothers and caregivers)! There are times when you can be very productive and get so much accomplished, yet never witness the sunrise or the beautiful sunset God created that day. Even at night when the stars are twinkling like sparkling diamonds against a pure black velvet background, you are inside trying to fix supper, help with homework, deal with issues, watch the news and unwind if that is possible. Then, before bed, you roll out the garbage, look up and marvel at God's creation, still on display. Another day has passed and the alarm will ring in the next one all too soon.

Sound familiar?

We all tend to struggle through life. As Christians, when the going gets tough, we go to God with our problems, thank Him for answered prayer, and immediately head out to fight the next battle on our own. We see ourselves on the frontlines, while God watches from the throne room waiting for a report, instead of realizing He goes before us.

Can you imagine if it were possible, to live inside your child, ready and able to go through anything with him, protecting him, guiding him, but never being acknowledged you were there? It would be totally frustrating if they only saw you as sitting home in front of the TV, waiting to hear of some problem you could solve. Or to be ignored and stand by while they struggled, were attacked by the enemy, or even worse, fell into sin and acted like you weren't there to help, especially knowing they will have to face the consequences.

This is often our mindset every day. Even when we have great devotional times in the morning, we often put away our Bibles, start our day and by 5:00 p.m. we are on our phone, rehashing the crisis of the day with our friends, family or colleagues, wondering how to handle it. Finally, we go to God and turn over the situation, knowing He can do all things. But we are exhausted in our spirit, worrying, retelling and trying to solve the problem first on our own.

Instead, we should live every day and every moment, in awe of our wonderful, indescribable, all powerful God who said "Let there be light" and there was light. The One who placed the stars in the sky and knows them all by name, made all things, gave us life, and redeemed us with the blood of His own Son, is the same God we invited into our humble hearts. *He lives inside our very being.* Can we comprehend that?

If we do, is there anything to fear? We may know it very well, but we fail to practice His presence. If we did, we would never worry, for He never fails. He promises to always work everything for the good for those who love Him and are called according to His purpose. Our name is engraved on the palm of His hand. His love is unfathomable. God wants us to know Him as our Heavenly Father, our Savior Jesus and our Counselor, the Holy Spirit. He is all we need. And it is His delight to give us the things we need most. He is the Good Shepherd who watches over His flock. Nothing can snatch us from His hand. If we drew near and talked to Him throughout our day, nothing would take us by surprise. We would be more aware that we are never alone and He is with us every moment. Even more important, we would be less likely to sin when tempted, realizing He was right there with us.

We need to draw near, not only to know when it is time to share our love story, but to remain witnesses for Him. If we fail to live out that life, we become hypocrites and it negates our testimony. Instead, we need to stay close, practice His presence, talk to Him daily and cherish our times alone with Him. He will give us a new word from scripture every day to take with us into battle.

I'm sure if you thought for a moment, you could name those you know who do practice His presence. They comfort others with the comfort they have been given. They seem to be towers of strength in times of trouble, yet their strength does not lie in their own frailty; they know how to trust God. Their love stories are based on solid truth, reflected in their lives day in and day out, not held together by loose threads. Because of His story, their lives were changed and they were never the same again.

It doesn't mean they don't make mistakes. They do, but they don't practice them. Even Paul said he fell time and again, but he got up, confessed and was once again renewed in God's presence.

We need to draw near and walk with our Lord moment by moment. Our days would take on new meaning as we learn to lean on Him in every circumstance. Isaiah 40:31 says "Those who hope in the Lord will renew their strength. They will soar on wings like eagles; they will run and not grow weary, they will walk and not be faint." If you walk daily with your hand in the Lord's, you would constantly be aware of the presence of His awesome power and know you are overwhelmingly covered in His unfailing love.

Draw near. He promises to draw near to you. When you practice His presence, you will not only recognize the opportunity of when, where and how to share your love story, you will live it every day, strengthened, refreshed and renewed in your Savior's arms.

**Class Discussion:**

1. Have you ever felt abandoned by God after you accepted Him as Savior? What was the result?

2. What do you feel will help you consider you are never alone?

3. Name a time when you truly sensed God's presence.

4. Give an example when you were led to share your love story and His timing was perfect.

# Chapter 5

# Know Your Public

$\mathscr{B}$efore you begin to openly share your love story, there's one thing you really need to be aware of - some people sing a totally different tune. In other words, they believe some pretty crazy stuff. I'm not just talking about being off a scripture or two; I'm talking aliens, Jesus and his brother Satan and the black hole. Of course, you really don't have to worry about such garbage, because you will be sharing the truth, but it isn't a bad idea to know your public.

If you aren't savvy to different faiths, I do not suggest you study them. First of all, it's a waste of time to study falsehood and if you are extremely naive the devil will take one untruth and twist your brain until you have spent several months down in a rabbit hole. If necessary, you can find a good reference at most any Christian bookstore. They have special colored foldout cards that outline different faiths as they pertain to Christianity. It's simple, easy and you can carry it in your Bible if need be. They often give scriptures from the Bible that directly negate each falsehood. If you try researching online, you will be reading for hours. Bottom line, the absolute best thing to do is to spend time in the Word, that way you will be armed for whatever is put before you. Often times a person will bring up something not even listed on the fold out. God knows just what you need. He never fails.

Now, let's talk about delivery. First and foremost, you are a child of God and if you are representative of Him (Who lives inside of you) you should act like one. It's been said that for some people you might be the only reflection of God they will ever see. Therefore, before ever saying a word, you should at least be an expression of His love. If you were asked to share your love story with someone at a certain time and a certain place, you would prepare yourself, mentally, spiritually, emotionally and physically. We don't always have that preparation time. Therefore, you could be asked to give it at any moment. You could be asked by a small child, or you could be asked by someone on their death bed. Be prepared, stay prepared. It could happen when you least expect it. Scripture says in 1 Peter 3:15, "But in your hearts revere Christ as Lord. Always be prepared to give an answer to everyone who asks you to give the reason for the hope that you have. But do this with gentleness and respect."

What if they are one of those who believe a far-fetched lie? First of all, we need to realize nobody follows something they think is totally untrue. If they are true followers of any belief, no matter how strange, they have made a rational decision beforehand to sign up. Others willingly join groups that are far out because they are rebelling from the norm. Whatever the case, they believe it. We have to remember one thing we all have in common...God loves us all the same. And moreover, Jesus died for the sins of the world. Don't let appearances fool you. Jesus loves them. If you have a chance to talk to someone who is asking you questions, look past their flesh and know their spirit is starving for truth.

Some people believe their faith IS Christian, just because it includes some form of "Jesus" but it isn't really the Jesus of the Bible. If you know the Word, you would recognize something immediately they believe is false. So how do you handle that? There is a saying that "The person who talks the most isn't always the person who is right." If you have the truth, you don't have to talk until you are blue in the face. The best thing to give them is scripture. If you stand on the truth, it can't be refuted. It's God's Word, not yours. Plus, when you have the answer, it doesn't have to be given flowery, or loudly. It can be simply stated with a smile. And that smile will reflect the Lord. Remember, if they differ in opinion or belief, they aren't rejecting you, they are rejecting Him.

If you attended the Sharing Your Love Story Workshop, you witnessed a short skit on "How Not to Witness." No one likes to be forced fed. Especially not a baby. Let the Spirit lead you. As indicated by the skit,

"The Right Way to Witness," there is a time you might be called to just be a helper, another time a giver, another time simply a listener and then a time to speak. We are not our own, so we need to follow the Spirit in each case. If God calls you only to listen, then do your best to listen as best you can. We are all part of one body and Christ is the Head.

Salvation work is His business and doesn't rest solely on our shoulders. The part we play is best done when He leads us to do it. He will open doors and shut others. He will open someone's heart, or they will shut the door to Him. It's not for us to decide, we just do what we are led to do.

Is there a time that we shouldn't say or do anything at all? Yes. Just because someone is totally lost, they could still be resolved in their heart that they are happy in their belief and don't want to hear anything about the truth. Later possibly, but for now, it's not the time to speak. We need to let them go and pray for them. The Holy Spirit still has work to do.

To sum it up, the best way to know your public is to know God first, what His Word says and be led by Him.

Class Discussion:

1. Share a time you were asked about your faith when you least expected it.

2. What is the most important thing we can do for those who are going the wrong way?

3. How can you be led by the Spirit to witness?

4. What's the best way to learn what someone else believes?

# Chapter 6

# Be Available

$\mathcal{S}$ometimes it seems like there aren't enough hours in the day. As I said in Chapter 1, there are days we don't see the sun rise or set and we still wonder how we possibly fit everything in. On a recent trip to Israel, I jumped out of my bed at 5:00 a.m., grabbed my IPAD and ran to the hotel balcony to take a video of the morning sun rising over the Sea of Galilee. It was amazing to watch that small glow on the horizon turn into a beautiful orange ball and finally bright yellow, as brilliant sunbeams glistened upon the same waves, I imagined the first apostles fished in the early dawn. Jesus must have watched that sunrise over 100 times while He was on earth and now, I was seeing it too. It was an overwhelming experience and definitely a "God Moment." Although I'm not a great photographer, I knew I had a once in a lifetime video. When I got back to the room I sat on the bed and prepared to watch it all over again. Much to my dismay, the video was nowhere to be found. Evidently, in my haste and excitement, I forgot to hit "save" on my IPAD. I was devastated. That was a tough lesson I learned to take time to do the things I do. I am always in far too much of a hurry. If I slowed down, I wouldn't miss some things that are truly important.

What about you? Would you want to lose an opportunity God gave you to share your love story? Someone could be right in front of you, eager to know the truth and accept Christ, and instead of paying attention, your mind is set on where you have to be next. Or even worse, you recognize it, but other pressing needs take priority. If someone asked you about Jesus, would you be willing to stop and put everything aside to tell them? Can God trust you to do that?

There seems to be an epidemic today of too many women who think they are suffering from dull and boring lives, when they are just sadly caught in the throes of routine living. For me, a life with Jesus Christ in the driver's seat has been anything but boring. Since the day He became Lord of my life, it's been an exciting journey on a bicycle built for two with Jesus on the front pedals. I have no idea where we are headed, I just know He is in charge and wherever we are going it has to be inspiring. My job is to just pedal in sync with Him. I can only glimpse at my journey from a peripheral view. I can tell we have gone up mountains and down valleys. The mountaintops have been glorious experiences, but there are times the valleys have been more than my heart could bear. Still, Jesus keeps pedaling forward, protecting me from harm, leading me where He wants me to go, always teaching me more about Him. It's been an amazing journey and I have to admit I have learned more in the valley than anywhere. It was in those darkest times I felt Him nearest me.

You are on the same ride I am. That is, of course, if you got on the bike. Some Christians accept Christ by opening their heart and then closing it to everything and everybody. They tuck Him away and call it "their personal faith." If the apostles felt that way, Christianity would have died over 2,000 years ago. Others happily get on but decide they feel safer in the driver's seat. They invite Jesus on THEIR bike and take Him wherever THEY go. They want to make sure He is there if anything goes wrong on their journey. He may be their Savior but not the Lord of their life.

That is not what salvation is all about. It is about turning your life over and letting Him be Master. I know I have gone over this before, but it bears repeating. What people don't realize is even if they don't get on the bike, life will take them places they never wanted to go. Right now, there are people all over the world who are lost, on the wrong road, and are in desperate need of direction. You and I have the answer but how do we know when, where and how to give it to them?

All three of these questions are answered easily. It's up to God, not you. He decides when, where and how. In your prayer time, tell Him you are willing to be used. Make yourself available. Then stay tuned to hear if He leads, be ready to be His vessel and listen for directions. While you are waiting, spend time with Him in His Word, learning more about Him. You will find answers to questions you haven't even been asked yet. The Holy Spirit will bring them to mind when you need them.

Jesus said in John 15:15, "I no longer call you servants, because a servant does not know his master's business. Instead I have called you friends, for everything that I learned from my Father I have made known to you." When you truly need a friend, don't you want them to be there for you? Jesus is always there for us. When He needs a friend, we need to be available for Him.

Witnessing is not scary or embarrassing. It is a divine appointment, set by God for someone to hear HIS love story. And the reason He is using you, is because you are available and your story was meant to touch theirs. At that moment, He is just asking for you to do exactly what He says. Be obedient. God does all the weaving in our lives and while we only see the loose threads under the tapestry, one day we will see the entire work. What an honor it is for Him to ask us to play a part. Let's not miss it. After all He has done for us, we should be shouting from the housetops. But let's leave that to the Holy Spirit. He knows just what to do.

## Class Discussion:

1. Have you ever told God you were willing to be His vessel?

2. How much fear is involved in sharing your faith if you are following God's instructions?

3. Share a time when you felt nearest to God.

4. How can you restructure your time to spend more of it with God?

# Appendix A

# The Roman Road

*Everyone needs salvation because we have all sinned.*

**Romans 3:10-12, and 23:** "As it is written: "There is no one righteous, not even one; there is no one who understands; there is no one who seeks God. All have turned away; they have together become worthless. There is no one who does good, not even one." "For all have sinned and fall short of the glory of God.""

*The price (or consequence) of sin is death.*

**Romans 6:23:** "For the wages of sin is death, but the gift of God is eternal life in Christ Jesus our Lord."

*Jesus Christ died for our sins. He paid the price for our death.*

**Romans 5:8:** "But God demonstrates his own love for us in this: While we were still sinners, Christ died for us."

*We receive salvation and eternal life through faith in Jesus Christ.*

**Romans 10:9-10, and 13:** "If you declare with your mouth, "Jesus is Lord," and believe in your heart that God raised him from the dead, you will be saved. For it is with your heart that you believe and are justified, and it is with your mouth that you profess your faith and are saved." "For everyone who calls on the name of the Lord will be saved."

*Salvation through Jesus Christ brings us into a relationship of peace with God.*

**Romans 5:1:** "Therefore, since we have been justified through faith, we have peace with God through our Lord Jesus Christ."

**Romans 8:1:** "Therefore, there is now no condemnation for those who are in Christ Jesus."

**Romans 8:38-39:** "For I am convinced that neither death nor life, neither angels nor demons, neither the present nor the future, nor any powers, neither height nor depth, nor anything else in all creation, will be able to separate us from the love of God that is in Christ Jesus our Lord."

**Steps to salvation:**

- Admit you are a sinner.

- Understand that as a sinner, you deserve death.

- Believe Jesus Christ died on the cross to save you from sin and death.

- Repent by turning from your old life of sin to a new life in Christ.

- Receive, through faith in Jesus Christ, his free gift of salvation.

Salvation prayer:

Dear God I confess to you that I am a sinner, and I am sorry for my sins; I need your forgiveness. I believe that your only begotten Son Jesus Christ shed His precious blood on the cross, died for my sins and rose from the dead. Please come into my heart, be my Savior and Lord of my life. Thank you for dying for me and giving me eternal life. In Jesus name, Amen.

# Appendix B

# How To Develop
# Your Love Story

In the Sharing Your Love Story Workshop, you were asked to fill in three boxes:

| Your life before Christ. | How you accepted Christ as your Savior. | Your life since you have accepted Him. |
|---|---|---|
| | | |

This is the easiest tool to use to expand your story. If you are speaking one on one, remember your shortened version is your main point. Bring that up first, and then revert back to the boxes, beginning with the one on the left. Consider your time. Get to the point. If you have more time, you can elaborate more, but always keep in mind to point to Christ, not yourself. Remember the person you are speaking to needs Christ, not you. You must explain what He did on the cross and how that made a difference in your life. No matter who they are or where they are in life, He is Who they need.

For those of you who are speaking to a group, the process is the same; however, you have to consider the exact time you been given. For instance, if you have 25 or 30 minutes, you can use five minutes to open with a funny story that will lighten your audience or say something by way of introduction that will build your life before Christ. Then get to your main point. Again, use the boxes as your guide allowing five minutes per box in this time frame. The last five minutes can be used to offer an invitation. Those details need to be worked out with the organization that invited you. Always follow the authority of the host that asked you to speak. Don't try to redo their methods. Spend time in prayer as you prepare your talk, while you travel and before you get up to deliver your testimony. God will give you peace and instead of being anxious you will enjoy the adventure of introducing others to Christ. It is truly an honor to do so.

Speakers are often asked for theme lines to use in advertising your attendance as guest speaker. Consider your main point and draw some type of wording from that. If there is a fashion show, you could use a theme that indicates you had a makeover in life or so on. There is no one better than God to give you creative ideas. Ask Him for what you need. He will lead you.

_**Most important to remember is this:**_ **there may be times when you are called to just give HIS story.** Someone could be in desperate need and want to know the truth and the truth alone. That is not a time to bring in your love story or what Jesus did for you. Focus on the gospel and as always use scripture. Don't be overbearing. Let the Spirit lead you. Share in love and offer them Jesus as the answer.

Discipleship is an important part of the salvation process. Those who have newly accepted Christ need to read their Bible, attend Church and fellowship with believers. This will help them to grow and not be choked out by the worries of the world. Instruct them to do so and pray for them as they begin their walk.

Finally, if you feel God leading you to speak in this area, or you would like to have a Sharing Your Love Story Workshop for your organization or church, feel free to contact me, I will be glad to assist you. You can email me at peachlane@bellsouth.net or call my cell, 985-630-1798. God Bless You!

Yours in Christ,

*Marlaine*

# Notes

CPSIA information can be obtained
at www.ICGtesting.com
Printed in the USA
FSHW010509040121
77382FS